FAITHWORKS

ImageWorks

PEOPLE INSTITUTE
Humanizing Business.Developing Relationships.

ISBN: 978-0-692-11463-6

First Edition: 2018

Design: Sara Martinez

FAITHWORKS

AN INNOVATIVE APPROACH
TO WORKFORCE DEVELOPMENT

CARLA HARRIS

Founder of ImageWorks Consulting Firm, LLC

ImageWorks

THE PEOPLE INSTITUTE

Humanizing Business.Developing Relationships.

WWW.ISYOURIMAGEWORKING.COM

Clients & Awards

Through ImageWorks, Carla Harris is considered a thought leader on the subject of Workforce Development training. Harris was recognized as a pioneer in the South Florida market, as the first image consultant to merge image consulting with professional development to assist transitioning and low-income job seekers.

ImageWorks' clients have included: the D.C. Department of Youth Rehabilitation Services; the D.C. Department of Employment Services; the National Center for Children and Families; Progressive Life Center, University of Miami; Holland & Knight; Paxen Group; the Salvation Army, National Capital Area Command; Peoria Workforce Network; South Florida Workforce; Baltimore County; Judicial College of Maryland; Maryland Association of Election Officials; and College Success Foundation.

Carla Harris' Awards and Honors have included:

*   Businesswoman of the Year—*South Florida Business Journal*
*   Finalist—Thelma Gibson Award of Excellence—Women's Chamber of Commerce of Miami-Dade County
*   Finalist—Up and Comers Award—*South Florida Business Journal*
*   Finalist—Outstanding Businesswoman of the Year—Coral Gables Chamber of Commerce

Carla Harris' community service has included:

*   Serving as Board Member and Youth Council Committee Chair for the South Florida Workforce (currently CareerSource South Florida) where she oversaw a $10M budget for programs and services to at-risk and underserved youth ages 18-24

- Chairman of the Board for the Women's Chamber of Commerce of Miami-Dade County—a business chamber of over 250 business members
- Board Member of the Miami-Dade Chamber of Commerce and Founding Chair of its Women's Council created to serve the woman-owned business leader
- Board Chair, Council for Workforce Development, Washington, DC
- Advisory Board Member, The Salvation Army National Capital Area Command, Washington, DC

ImageWorks' Outcomes and Achievements have included:

- Providing career development training and employment services to job seeking Candidates aged 50 and older through the Alternative Pathways Employment Program
- Providing Workforce Development to adjudicated youth ages 18-21 in career readiness and occupational skills training with a job placement rate of 60%
- Serving more than 4,500 TANF recipients and at-risk youth in Miami, Florida from 2000-2005—88% program completion rate
- Developing a mentor/mentee program for Steel, Hector and Davis law firm matching adjudicated male students from an alternative high school with attorneys and paralegals—Miami, Florida
- Creating a pilot job readiness program for 50 displaced professionals as part of the Rapid Response initiative in Peoria, Illinois in 2003—100% program completion rate

Dedication

This book is dedicated to all the Candidates I've had the pleasure of meeting since beginning my journey in Workforce Development. Your journey is not without fear, trepidation and rounding corners you're not quite sure of. Always surround yourself with people who want you to be your best. Success is yours for the taking.

Acknowledgements

With special thanks to God. Without faith, I simply don't know where I'd be.

Thank you to my beautiful daughter Nina. I know it's hard being the child of a solo-*Mom-preneur*, but you are a trooper and I am so proud to be your mom.

Thank you to my parents—June and Pleasant Harris—who taught me that kindness comes first.

Thanks to my village—you know who you are—for helping me through my journey.

Thank you to Tara...you know why!

Finally, thank you for the unconditional love and support of my brother Peter J. Harris. Ma and Daddy are smiling down and seeing something GREAT! I love you for your sibling love and adult friendship.

You'll Never Hear Someone Say: 'I'm Absolutely Sick and Tired of Respect and Recognition'

You'll Never Hear Someone Say: 'I'm Absolutely Sick and Tired of Respect and Recognition'

By Thomas A. Gordon, Ph.D.
Principal, Thomas A. Gordon & Associates
Philadelphia, PA

In 2017, I spoke with my close friend, Peter Harris, founder Black Man of Happiness Project (www.blackmanofhappiness.com). In conversation, Peter introduced Carla Harris, his sister; offering to bridge me to Carla. He touched lightly on Carla's brilliance, professional expertise, and strong work ethic. He spoke passionately about her character, commitment to develop, serve, and empower vulnerable citizens, and refusal to straddle or excuse or settle for anything less than execution excellence.

Peter spoke about Carla's leadership, ethical compass, and heart. Before I had met Carla or read *FaithWorks*, Peter had helped me to hear Carla's vision, voice, the dysfunctional systemic and transactional patterns she had already peeped, and the desired, more collaborative future she envisioned.

There is a better way—for us to be better persons, better people, and better professionals. We can and must change. We can choose better life-advancing, life-affirming workforce development and human service institutions, programs, career pathways, systems, and mutually beneficial supports. *FaithWorks* articulates, amplifies, and illuminates that better way.

FaithWorks reintroduces and reinvigorates in-depth reflection on, not just important job and career-building matters, but the foundational question of what it means to be faithfully, authentically, and fully human— with all the rights, privileges, active accountabilities, role responsibilities, systemic barriers, historical/habitual burdens, toxic judgments, and rules of constructive vs. mutually marginalizing engagement that entails.

Carla Harris challenges, provokes, invites, and guides us to consider what human talent and potential we might together develop, achieve, and deliver—we professionals who shift into 24/7/365 "professing," modeling, and caring enough to bring empowering principles and practices as well as we help seeking "Candidates" or service recipients who show up, often marginalized, bruised, and baggage-heavy, to negotiate routinely inhospitable, impersonal institutions for practical survival and life opportunities. We, together, can and must change, intelligently adapt, feed our transformative faith, love, respect, and focus.

If we structure, reposition, resource, and reclaim human beings as centric to human success—as inherently deserving and worthy of welcome, warmth, practical guidance, self-mastery support, restorative discipline, material access, and empowering respect, *FaithWorks* argues that we disruptively and constructively shift human service delivery for the better. In a USA society that treats marginalized human beings as permanently burdensome, deficient commodities and consumers, *FaithWorks* advocates developing human potential anyway, boosting systemic respect anyhow, humanizing workforce service policies and practices, and recasting service recipients as "Candidates" and "partners" for mutually beneficial exchange. To know better is to be and do better.

Faith without work is dead. Love directs and fuels the work. *FaithWorks* testifies for love energy—and all of its respectful, practical, even tough love, derivatives.

Let's not just chase job placement transactions and routines. Let's not just go through the self-serving motions of processing and paperwork rituals. Let's not match present dysfunction with past dysfunction, again and again. Let's not treat real human beings with real world challenges as deeply, irreparably flawed dead-ends. Let's define a better way.

Love, practical, customized, and applied, is indispensable to human success. Respect, a transformative love-derivative, is always high impact fuel for superior human development, collaboration, and productive thriving. You'll never hear someone say: I'm absolutely sick and tired of respect and recognition—I have too much of it.

Nina Simone once said: "You have to learn to get up from the table when love is not being served."

Carla Harris champions more practical, life-advancing, capacity-building love for the meal—resetting the menu, mindset, manners, demeanor, and engagement excellence to, ultimately, transform the human services table.

◊ ◊ ◊

Thomas A. Gordon, Ph.D., is founder and principal of TAGA Consulting. For some 40 years, Gordon has been a college professor, health and mental health systems manager, psychotherapist, leadership coach, and organizational advisor. He has provided strategic counsel to Fortune 500 enterprises, executives globally, as well as to organizations in the public, education, healthcare, aerospace, defense, insurance, legal, manufacturing, and telecommunications sectors.

A More
Humane Way

A More Humane Way

By Carla Harris

For me, Workforce Development is personal. It's a mission that drew me in. It was not a chosen path.

I believe that the work, which chose me, has made me a better person. Made me see clearly that there is a better way.

There is the human way—a more humane way!

I have been the Candidate. I have been the Provider. What separates us? Nothing.

I will never forget the feeling of sitting across the desk from a case manager, her facial expressions and tone of voice signaling that I was lazy, with nothing to offer, while she interviewed me about why I needed public assistance.

I remember thinking…wow! And they call this social *service?*

It's that memory that makes me an advocate for my Candidates.

It's that memory that makes me want to 'Humanize Human Services.'

It's that memory that makes me want to propose a new way of serving fellow citizens in need.

It's that memory that motivates me to outline a comprehensive vision of service, to analyze the language of Workforce laws, to challenge professional leadership of state and local agencies, and to ask fundamental questions about how frontline staff interact with men and women seeking services.

At ImageWorks, we want agencies to realize it's not about them.

It's about the 'humans' embedded in such official titles as Department of HUMAN Services.

Also, we want an employer to realize that Candidates recruited from a 'government funded program' are like anyone seeking a job.

They will need training and must meet the specs of job descriptions. But guess what?

EVERY new employee requires training and must meet the specs of job descriptions.

Honestly, I cannot say that I've helped everyone I've worked with as a Workforce Development professional.

But I can honestly tell you that each Candidate with whom I've worked has changed my life immensely.

I carry a part of them with me. A memory. I love my Candidates.

For me this is personal.

Sometimes we are chosen to do something that is so far from our own desire that we are not even sure it's the right thing.

That is what Workforce Development has become for me.

But when I think about it, it really isn't that farfetched. Helping people be their best has always been a part of my calling, whether I'm working as an image consultant, serving members of my church congregation, teaching staff development courses, or sponsoring a conference on hiring folks who've found themselves on the 'sidelines' of society.

Like all difficult challenges, especially public policy challenges, 'Humanizing Human Services' will be demanding.

We'll have to review and revise some of our cherished (and often calcified) beliefs about ourselves and the folks sitting across from us.

In FaithWorks, I hope that by sharing my journey, and the rationales for my vision, I will spark a national conversation about changing human services for the betterment of our fellow citizens in transition.

And beyond discussion, I pray we'll ACT on the highest principles whenever we find ourselves charged to help find work for that person sitting across from us.

Always remembering, 'There but for the grace of God....'

CHAPTER ONE

Working
the Image

Working the Image

Image is everything. I've always believed that. I've always believed that having the right image meant being appropriately dressed for whatever the occasion. As founding CEO of ImageWorks Consulting Firm, LLC, my innovative Workforce Development company, I must sometimes overcome what I hope folks perceive as an impeccable image. Sometimes, I might have to push back against assumptions about who I am and how I roll. I might have to heighten a dramatic moment with a shocking gesture.

And what is *Carla Harris' image?*

I think I can confidently say, first and foremost, that I'm rigorously professional, stylishly appropriate. The right clothes. The right make-up. Prepared, always prepared. No-nonsense, but full of laughter. Oriented toward the bottom line. But I love to negotiate for mutual benefits. I'm a Workforce Development professional, whose faith inspires me to incorporate *love* into my advocacy for the men and women I serve. Also, I'll admit, I can be a demanding taskmaster.

Furthermore, I've learned that it's important that I lead with my image with everyone I meet—my many collaborators and the business partners with whom I negotiate.

When I walk out of the house I *am* an image. My image is my brand. I walk the walk and talk the talk. I'm as comfortable in the *'Hood* as I am in the White House.

But sometimes, I've learned, in order to increase my effectiveness, my ability to make my image the most effective tool it can be, I have to step *beyond* my image, step from behind my carefully constructed public presentation.

Like that time when some of my younger clients, court-supervised youth ....

Wait a minute....

Let's first get the terminology right. In our Workforce Development division, ImageWorks doesn't serve *Clients*, *Returning Citizens*, *At-Risk Youth*, or *Underserved Populations!*

We work with Candidates. With a Capital C!

At ImageWorks, we call the folks we serve Candidates—as in *Job Candidates.*

Agencies call them customers; they're not customers; they're not buying anything! Participants? What are they participating in? Some of it's so insulting. It's another way of looking at a person as a number. *Ultimately, in the big scheme of things, we want to humanize human services!* Ironically our work is called human services. We want to inspire or instruct agencies to view their Candidates as people, as human beings in need, folks who certainly need help—sometimes quick, fast and in a hurry.

But in truth, for real, each Candidate is a citizen who deserves respect from a publicly funded agency. I mean that each Candidate should find respect from every level of the agency. Candidate walks in the door. He should be respected by the administrative and security staff. Candidate asks questions about her paperwork, she should be respected by the person handing out paperwork. And listen, I have been at this long enough to know that in some cases the young woman handing out the paperwork may herself have just graduated from a social service program; indeed, her salary may be partially subsidized by Workforce Development funds.

And once a Candidate gets *processed*, well then, Counselors and Case Workers must provide support respectfully. They must be reflections of respect sent down from Supervisors. All staff must be reflections of the policy set by the agency director.

I want to see respect baked into Workforce Development legislation. I want respect to collapse the distance between a Candidate and any publicly funded position, federal, state and local! Agency director. Politician. Legislative Staff. They cannot *feel* so far removed from the lives of our Candidates that they reduce them to *clients*.

OK, ok, I'm sorry. I veered off there didn't I?!

Let me take a deep breath. I have to laugh at myself. It's a knowing laugh, a self-deprecating laugh, at how my 'On-the-Clock Expert' can take over the flow of my most intimate storytelling. *Madam Expert* is the leader my Candidates see. The innovative leader. The blunt leader. Their advocate who sometimes puts aside subtlety, as I go hard on their behalf. The one they call a respectful Miss Harris. The passionate lady who'll cut her eyes at you, if you don't remove your hat as you're entering the office. The inspiring Miss Harris, who'll pull you aside and jump in your face if you're bringing too much street into the suites.

No question *Madam Expert* took me off track!

◊ ◊ ◊

So let me get back to that time I was sitting with my younger Candidates.

...They were complaining. It was a pretty big group, probably about 14 or 15 young men and women. We were doing an exercise about answering interview questions. We were all in a circle, in which we throw a small ball and whoever caught the ball has to answer questions. It was at the end of the day. What were they complaining about?

'*I can't get a job.*'

'*You don't understand.*'

'*The agency is lying to us.*'

'*Y'*all *are lying to us.*'

'*You said you were going to give us a job.*'

While they were complaining, I got up from the circle. I went to my office. I got my card. I came back to the circle. I gave the card to one of the Candidates. Told him to pass it around and take a look at it. As the card was going around, I asked, 'Whose name is on it?' They slowly realized it was *my* Capital Care EBT card, the card on which the government loads cash and food benefits. I shared highlights of my story, about my time moving from Miami back home to D.C., when I was in my transition, after a divorce, raising my first child alone, when I couldn't find a job, when I didn't have enough capital to set up ImageWorks, and I was having to use the system.

And everybody got quiet. There was just silence, because they all know what it means to have an EBT card. I wanted to remove the shadow, the myth, that Miss Harris has got it all together, all the time. I wanted them to know that I had worked for it and 'you can work for it too.' I wanted to strip a layer from myself. I wanted them to know I don't have anything to hide. I wanted my Candidates to know another side of me, that part of my life, which is not their *image* of me. Which is not part of the image I've developed.

So yes, I know my image! My image is my brand. An EBT card is not a part of my brand. I know that. But people don't know that, because I know how to do Image well. I walk the walk and talk the talk. I think passing around the EBT card really kind of humanized me in the eyes of our Candidates who could only see the result of all my hard work.

Circulating an EBT card I used during one the deepest valleys in my life! That was hard, but that was classic *Madam Expert*—although softened to connect with my young folks. But they had to be checked in a way they would viscerally understand. Circulating that card was a silent, powerful testimony that stripped away all excuses any of them might float in their frustration, misery, poverty, anger, and paralysis.

Circulating that card challenged those young folks. Demanded they peep their patterns, accept all the responsibility they can shoulder, re-frame their problems, and shift their energies from complaining to collaborating, driven by their most important dreams of a life well lived.

I told them that afternoon, and I will tell any Candidate, heads of government agencies, and anyone else who will listen:

Workforce Development is about understanding the true core of a person and helping them make a career.

And it takes learning and executing the choreography of really, really hard work, resilience, planning, and teamwork—by both the Candidates and the Workforce Development agencies and organizations which serve them.

I'm really tired of working with Candidates the way it's always been done. I think this fear within the system as a whole has set up the people for failure. The whole system. We live in a very reactive instead of proactive system. Instead of really thinking it through and laying out an entire program, one that's age-friendly, that's thought-out fully from the top down, agencies sometimes throw programs together. Sometimes in 3 weeks! Without really understanding the full implications of telling Candidates, 'get a job; we'll pay you; you have support for one year.' And what the Candidate heard was, 'one year and get paid'—thinking they're going to get paid a full year to look for a job....

What the agency should say, especially to contractors such as ImageWorks, is this: We're choosing you to be our partner; let's talk about how we're going to roll it out *before* we roll it out. Let's discuss issues, expectations, goals. Let's run scenarios in which we anticipate the reactions of Candidates facing various situations confronting them. Let's assess our assumptions. Let's discern how we serve Candidates at different life-stages.'

For example, more mature Candidates may have more work experience, but they may not be as qualified as they assert when, say, describing their digital skill set. Are they savvy when using email programs? Do they regularly check their emails? What if their phones are disconnected? How does Workforce training take this into account without holding the hands of Candidates? How does Workforce training lead Candidates to remain accountable, while teaching them to manage difficult or challenging situations? As planning partners, we'd bring deep knowledge of our Candidates, without sugar coating the challenges we all face.

Those challenges are real for Candidates. These challenges—especially for younger men and women—can land them in jail. Or can be fatal.

◊ ◊ ◊

Recently, I learned that one of our younger Candidates, TB (not his real name), one of the guys I really love, who had, *who has*, so much potential, is in jail on federal felony charges, because *he was in a shoot-out!* Not just shooting up in the air. *He was in a shoot-out in D.C.*

Whether I am Madam Expert, or Miss Carla, the advocate and educator, the fierce professional and the dedicated protector, surprise reversals such as losing one of my guys to prison, keeps me sober. Reminds me that humanizing human services is not just idealism. Real lives are at stake.

Here at ImageWorks they guide us through them steps
They put us on the straight and narrow path for success...
And all through the week / yeah they coaching and they prep
So on that final day / man they wishing us the best
That's ImageWorks / I'm shinin / I'm ballin...
That's ImageWorks / I'm working / I'm learning

Those lyrics, written by our younger Candidates as part of a team-building project, inspire me to think, tragically, about another young guy. A few years ago, I got a phone call from the friend of another promising young man named M. I was told that M was killed. He was shot execution style in Barry Farms. Took my breath away. Still takes my breath away. One step forward. Two steps backwards. I was so disappointed. I mean, my hope is that our younger Candidates' experience with ImageWorks will lead them to think, 'Man, they sure got on my nerves, but everything they did was for my own good.' I hope they will gain skills, connections, and jobs that will take them off the firing line.

Then I was disappointed that the *system* is so screwed up and is so shortsighted. When M was killed, it was within 6 to 9 months after we worked with him under a one-year contract with the D.C. government. Because of funding cuts, our contract was not renewed. And because ImageWorks is a small organization, we couldn't continue the daily support he needed. M had been with us for just under a year. I knew that we were close to a breakthrough with him. We placed him on a job. He was working on a construction site. The people were very complimentary of him. He wanted to do more with himself. So the contract ends, and because we're a small business, we can't continue the support. If only we had another year with him. If only we were able to maintain that steady contact. If only...

So back to this *latest* news about TB. When he's released, it will be close to impossible for him to get a job! It's literally almost impossible for him to be hired by the time he is released. I've had this discussion with the powers that be. Very clearly, there has to be a longer contract cycle. Of course, put agency monitoring into the longer contract. Of course, mandate site visits in the longer contract. Fiscal and service audits. Of course.

I am a big girl. I welcome the monitoring. I know my records are rigorous. Send over the inspectors. A longer contract just means ImageWorks, and other contracted providers, will have a longer timeline of positive performance measures. AND we get longer to serve and guide our Candidates. We get longer to break negative circuits in their lives. Coach them through the landmines in their lives. Longer contract is classic win-win. We get stronger cash flow and our Candidates benefit from our ability to provide persistent services.

You *cannot* facilitate change in one year, especially when you're taking a person who is 18, 19, 20, who's had 18, 19, 20 years of being told, 'You ain't worthy! You ain't going to be anything!' It takes two years just to re-do the thinking. You're really re-conditioning a thought process.

From a Workforce Development perspective, Candidates feel they face disrespect from so many directions. And short contracts are another systemic form of disrespect. At ImageWorks, I really understand what's it like being on the other side of the desk. Too many at the contracting agencies are not 'bilingual' in this manner. Like I said: I'm as comfortable in the *Hood* as I am in the White House. I'm a straight shooter. I don't like to sugar coat things—probably to a fault.

But I know I can't be sitting up in the tower and not know what's going on in the trenches. We need performance worthy of measure. You cannot make this a numbers' games for the Candidates we're talking about. You cannot release somebody from jail on Friday and put them in Workforce Development on Monday. They've got to sow their oats. I say take two weeks; do what you want—*except put yourself back in jail!* But when you come to ImageWorks, be ready to work. That approach illustrates a process in which people come first.

Tragically, and believe me I am quite clear on this point, learning about my journey won't change some Candidates at all. I've seen it in some of the Candidates that I've worked with over the years. They think: 'Success will never happen to me.' They are trapped by a self-defeating kind of thinking. 'You did it Miss Harris, but I can't do it.' They make assumptions. In their self-denial, they say to themselves, 'You're successful, but it's never been as bad for you as it has been for me.' Too often, Candidates believe the successful person has not faced challenges as harsh as theirs. Or they doubt their own intestinal fortitude. They don't feel they have the same *go-gettedness* of a person who has succeeded.

So, I struggle to remain flexible, seeking the effective blend between the personal and the professional.

Miss Harris serves our Candidates with as much stamina and imagination as I can bring to bear, even if it means passing around an expired EBT card from my time in the 'trenches.'

Madam Expert walks the halls of human service agencies with as much savvy and innovation as my Workforce Development experiences allow me to wield.

And I speak my mind and describe my visions. I keep my eyes on the prize to ensure that our Candidates don't find themselves permanently on the margins and sidelines of our society.

'It's Not Easy, But It's Doable'

*Carla Harris' speech at Alternative Pathways
to Employment Program Graduation
September 16, 2016*

...Working with this first cohort of 29 people has been exciting, fulfilling and sometimes a bit exhausting. When we met this first group of nervous, unsettled and unemployed Candidates, we were greeted with trepidation, nervousness about what to expect, and fear of the unknown. Many of them came to us with a personal expectation of what it means to find employment and how to do it. They quickly found out that finding employment first begins with finding ourselves.

It was our job to set the ground rules and to create an environment where it was okay to be afraid, to ask questions, and to *not know what you don't know!* In fact, one of the first exercises asked: 'What did you want to be when you grew up?' For many of them, that was the first time they'd given that question any thought in a very long time. At ImageWorks, our philosophy is to ask *Why*? Why do you want to be the doctor, the police officer, the teacher, the nurse, the chef...? Find the why and you will find the foundation of the reason you seek certain types of employment.

During the first 2 weeks, we did not talk about resumes, how to interview, how to dress, or what to say during a salary negotiation. What we did was explore the WHY of wanting to work, and how to find the work that brings joy. Our Candidates wrote a personal manifesto that defined goals for the next 12, 18, and 24 months, with a broad overview of the next 5 years.

I've been told that we have created 'monsters' and raised the bar too high. And yes, I will admit that our style of career coaching and professional development is to teach others to do what they believe in and to do it well. To find what makes their heart sing. In addition, we teach them how to create a career path based on taking what you love and paring it down to its lowest common denominator, and if you don't have the skills needed to do the "perfect" job, to gain employment in a related field.

Workforce Development requires action, innovative thinking, realistic expectations and time. It also requires networking and an ability to create relationships with all kinds of people. More than 65% of all jobs are NOT ADVERTISED; that said, networking is a vital part of our Workforce Development program. Developing a LinkedIn page and then using it to sell yourself; using it to network with others and to reach out to those companies you WANT to work with. Real-time networking is also a valuable skill—ImageWorks hosted a private meet-and-greet reception; we also create other opportunities to network by inviting our Candidates to events we produce.

> ## *Workforce Development requires action, innovative thinking, realistic expectations and time.*

Finding employment is a full-time job. The average time to complete an online application is 90 minutes and involves editing your resume, researching the company and evaluating the salary opportunities to ensure it's a good fit—and that's all before you press send.

At ImageWorks, Workforce Development is personal. I have been in your seat. I have needed to figure out my Why? I have been where you are. It's not easy, but it's doable.

WHO DO WE SERVE?

Key Challenges facing ImageWorks'
Workforce Development Candidates

YOUNG COHORT [18-24 years of age]

- Disengaged Emotionally and Socially
- Living in underserved neighborhoods
- Caring for younger siblings or their own children
- Setting Unrealistic goals
- Lacking self awareness
- Doubting personal potential
- Lacking motivation
- Claiming negative youth culture: e.g. adopting one image in the *Hood*, one image on the job
- Possessing poor communication skills
- Required to contribute income to family
- Feeling entitled to services
- Serving under court supervision
- Failing to re-acclimate to family and adjust to life outside prison walls
- Tempted or trapped by *The Life*

MATURE COHORT

- Overwhelmed by demands of today's work requirements
- Lacking motivation to adapt to current situation and era
- Lacking tech skills
- Feeling their work experience entitles them to preferential treatment
- Feeling their work experience entitles them to Workforce Development
- Possessing poor communication skills

No Margins,
No Sidelines

CHAPTER TWO

No Margins, No Sidelines

How can citizens living on the margins, living on the sidelines, benefit from the national shift from welfare to Workforce Development?

Since this big shift started during the Clinton Administration in the 1990s, answering that crucial question has driven and motivated me.

I support the ideal 'win-win' of that shift:

Folks get weaned off public assistance; folks receive training for work; folks get employed at living wages. At the same time, society welcomes the energy, ideas and vitality of motivated workers new to the workforce; the economy expands thanks to the circulation of increased wages and spending; and government budgets receive a jolt of increased tax receipts. And look, for the most part, Workforce Development Candidates just want an opportunity to get a job to be able to take care of their family.

But my experience has identified a core Workforce Development challenge: lacking an "Emotional Intelligence." And too often, the gap doesn't register for providers, who face their own legal demands to get 'em in and get 'em out!

Here are some fundamentals. Candidates have to change. The law says you start with 60 months in the bank—5 years, unless you have extenuating circumstances, a disability or something like that.

Seems like enough time to get trained and find a job, right? Seems like enough time to treat people with dignity and with respect, and craft a plan that takes into account what most Candidates face as they manage the transition from public assistance to gainful employment.

But too many Workforce Providers—from agency directors to front-line staff—create what feels like a threatening environment, in which, ironically, getting a job is the *only* clear, legally mandated, goal.

Threatening doesn't mean effective. Furthermore, it's not touchy-feely to build relationships into the process guiding how staff and the Candidates can work together.

Establishing rich human connections must stop being bad-mouthed as 'soft skills.' You better understand what drives a Candidate! How can you create an effective training and job-search plan without recognizing and respecting Candidates' fears, social pressures, even years of self-sabotaging patterns? How can providers be their most effective without *simultaneously* recognizing and addressing their own preconceptions, biases, mixed signals, and tendencies to impose one-size-fits-all strategies?

Of course, it's not a simple nor static process. But it's a process that *must* honor the complex dynamics of working with real people in an effort to help them secure real jobs. Real people, American citizens, who are caught in the gears of a society struggling with a huge shift in policies designed to serve the most vulnerable, who often lack the personal and political muscle to influence that shift in any way!

When President Bill Clinton signed the Personal Responsibility and Work Opportunity Reconciliation Act (PRWORA) of 1996, it replaced the Aid to Families with Dependent Children (AFDC) program, in effect since 1935, and the Job Opportunities and Basic Skills Training (JOBS) program of 1988. PRWORA shifted from Federal payments directly to citizens, to a block grant program allowing states to design their own systems while meeting a set of core federal requirements.

Basically, the legal change required that folks on 'welfare' had to go to work; they had to begin working after two years of receiving benefits; and they had a lifetime limit of five years on benefits paid by federal funds. Also, PRWORA enhanced the enforcement of child support paid by noncustodial parents. Overall, states could distribute federal money in different ways. Some states emphasized education, others helped fund private enterprises helping job seekers.

It was a 'work first' initiative. Every single person needed to get a job or they were going to lose their benefits. Companies said, 'You gotta be kidding! *They* don't show up to work on time—if they come to work at all! They don't communicate well. They bring all their baggage to work, all their home drama. They don't know how to dress or present themselves professionally.' Lawmakers and policy wonks went back in the huddle and said, 'We got to figure this out.'"

The year 1998 brought the Workforce Investment Act (WIA), which superseded the Job Training Partnership Act (JTPA) and amended the Wagner-Peyser Act. WIA also contains the Adult Education and Family Literacy Act (Title II) and the Rehabilitation Act Amendments of 1998 (Title IV).

Then everybody was getting training, but weren't getting any jobs. So politicians go back into the huddle; they come out of the huddle and they say, 'We have to train them, but they have to be trained in a high-demand occupation,' which is whatever is supporting the economy in your region. For example, in DC, or CA that might be IT, Information Technology. In other areas, it might have been health care. The thinking was that it didn't make any sense to train someone how to be a forklift operator somewhere there weren't a lot of those jobs. I was in Miami in those days, so obviously training for tourism and hospitality were priorities.

With the Obama Administration, in 2015, WIA was superseded by the Workforce Innovation and Opportunity Act (WIOA), "designed to help job seekers access employment, education, training, and support services to succeed in the labor market and to match employers with the skilled workers they need to compete in the global economy," according to the US Department of Labor website.

So now there's an intertwinement of education and employment. If a person wants to be a Registered Nurse, and he or she wants to go to school, it will be paid for as part of a career-training plan. Say your first job requires a Home Health Aide certification; next you'll get paid to study for your CNA (Certified Nursing Assistant) Certification. Your next course is maybe to become a medical technician; and theoretically, if you're working for a company like Kaiser, each of these courses of study should build on the other at that company. All of your studies should be aligning your career goals and your education goals to get where you really want to be. It's working but it's a long process.

On the other side, the company employing Candidates receive a tax credit, because Candidates come from an underserved community or an at-risk demographic and have been receiving some kind of government assistance. The company's thinking is this: 'If I'm hiring you as a Home Health Aide, but I think you have the potential to become a CNA, I'll pay for your education and the government will reimburse me up to 75 percent.' The employer gets to train or retrain a person; and the Candidate gets support to work and leave public assistance, and it all takes place as part of a rational process that takes a Candidate's needs and goals into account.

Whatever the law, if the goal is to convert folks receiving public assistance into gainfully employed citizens, then the Workforce Development process requires respect for a delicate balance. Workforce Development professionals, and here I include national, state, and local lawmakers, agency directors, and their staff members, must be more than bureaucrats reacting to changing political climates.

In the trenches, where the laws are executed, there remains a need to keep front-and-center the humanity and individuality of the Candidates—no matter how dizzying the powerful political pressures, the on-going calibration of federal and local laws and politics, and the shifting blend of procedures, plans, strategies, and evaluations.

For example, the leaders and legislators are educated. They're typically not substance abusers. For the most part, they don't have criminal backgrounds. They have motivation. A strong support system. Desire. Legislators make rules based on what they know. There are people, too often, sitting in their towers making rules that affect people who often *don't* have motivation, *don't* have the support system, who may have been abused for years.

If we're not careful as a society, this gap can widen into an insurmountable chasm. There's such a big disparity between what's real and what the policies say you should be doing. They are policies based on legislators' frame of reference. If agencies humanize their process, actual Candidates—the end user of policies—would be more receptive to the change.

Humanizing human services is a mind-set, guiding actions that will, with strategic thinking, and a lot of hard work, transform our Workforce Development system from an ineffective maze into an interconnected web.

Proposing & Executing Innovation

Excerpts of ImageWorks Correspondence

PROPOSING INNOVATION TO PROSPECTIVE CLIENT

Thank you for taking the time to meet last week. You gave me lots to think about. Per our discussion, we left the following open: Corporate Training for your team—as I mentioned, we don't subscribe to "cookie-cutter" training approaches. That said, I'd like you to think about the following questions so we can best serve the needs of your company. You mentioned that you'd like to establish a *Core Culture* in your company. Your answers to the following questions will help us create the right professional development programs for your staff:

1. What does service mean to you as the leader of your company? I'd like you to take our service assessment and candidly assess where you believe your team is and where you want them to be.
2. What words would you use to describe the *Core Culture* of your company? What words do you believe *your team* would use to describe the culture? What is your goal for your company—in the community, in the corporate sector, from your clients' perspective?
3. What are the three areas that are keeping you and your team from reaching the goals you've set?
4. How could ImageWorks' new *Hiring from the Sidelines* program for workforce professionals help contribute to the creation of your firm's Core Culture?
5. How could your new Core Culture help put the "human" back in human services?

EXECUTING INNOVATION
To A Government Agency

...Your letter indicates that *'your firm failed to perform as required by the subject contract providing work-based training for 22 participants....'* To date, 24 participants are either in work-based training or unsubsidized employment. We will address each of the deficiencies you noted:

ImageWorks failed to provide clear and consistent programming which resulted in the disengagement of 12 program participants following the provision of work readiness services. ImageWorks was contracted to provide job readiness training to youth ages 14 and 15. We were able to start the program within ten days of the initial conversation. Likewise, we were contacted about another urgent need to provide services to [mature workers]. Again, ImageWorks started the program three days later. [Even with] less than three weeks [lead time, ImageWorks was] told by the Director's office "to make it happen." ImageWorks was not a part of the planning discussions, nor a part of the screening process of the participants—some of whom have no GED/HS Diploma, no current technological skills, and unrealistic expectation from the existing job market.

ImageWorks provided [your office and Candidates with] very clear and consistent program details. We made it very clear on the day of orientation in the presence of all staff and program participants that our focus was 'career readiness' and what that entailed. We were also clear that we do not 'guarantee' employment, since we could not dictate to an employer who to hire; we could not require Candidates to accept positions; and we could not exit participants from the program. For the past 17 years this has been our philosophy about the Workforce Development training we provide. Our outline [indicated] that we would prepare Candidates how to be successful employees; how to successfully re-enter the workplace through effective career pathway planning; and how to interact with employers and co-workers in the workplace.

Our *Building a Successful Image for Change* program is a comprehensive career readiness and coaching program and has been since its inception. Additionally, as a regular part of our programming, we ask participants to complete an anonymous program evaluation; we were highly rated (scored 8 or higher) by more than 78% of those who completed the evaluation....

ImageWorks' strategy to introduce Candidates to employers has been successful in this program. In October, we hosted two events—a Candidate showcase and an employer-networking event. During the Candidate showcase, seven Candidates were offered employment and five declined the offer of unsubsidized employment, with benefits, because the salary was not what they were "accustomed to." Additionally, two other Candidates were offered second interviews; one was offered employment and she remains employed to this day.

Finally, to provide additional context, the program, which was a pilot, was put together in a very short period and has had three leadership changes within [your agency] in eight months. This has caused communication challenges with ImageWorks, as providers, as well as the participants, who have also undergone multiple changes in coaches and case managers. As a result, communication and expectations have been a challenge throughout the life of the program.

Our goal at ImageWorks is to serve job seekers and help them prepare for navigating the workplace. Our experience in working with [your agency] has been extraordinary considering both contracts were of an urgent nature—and one was a pilot—and both were put in place by ImageWorks within ten days of initial communication from [your agency]. We remain committed to the work we do and to finding a mutually satisfactory resolution to the concerns you've presented.

Sincerely,
Carla Harris, CEO

CHAPTER THREE

Rising in Faith

Rising in Faith

Every day, I'm strengthened by my personal faith, in God, in the truth of my own experience. And I know this simple truth: Once you fall, you don't have to stay there! My *faith* is my rock—my living, breathing foundation, from which I can be creatively *rock-steady*. From my foundation, I humanize the services provided by ImageWorks. Simultaneously, I infuse services with tough-love, sensitive understanding of the dynamic Workforce Development field, and applied expertise of the local economic landscape.

Let me reiterate, and dig deeper, into my contention that humanizing human services is not touchy-feely. Compassion is *not* touchy-feely. *Respect* is *not* touchy-feely. Neither are *encouragement* and *inspiration!* They are, in fact, very effective Workforce Development tools. They are not, in fact, so-called 'soft skills'.

I have wielded those tools. I have been a beneficiary of professionals who've used those tools. And with ImageWorks, we craft approaches to serving Candidates that rest on, and wisely blend, the use of those tools, based on rigorous assessments of each individual's needs, dreams, and visions.

I am *not* advocating missionary work with ImageWorks' Candidates. Far from it. No, I'm advocating that we trust in the simple truth that Candidates come to human service agencies imbued with their own powerful faiths, their own powerful experiences, and their own powerful motivations.

Guided by this concept, ImageWorks respectfully meets Candidates where they are. Helps them assess their skills. And we absolutely check a half-stepping Candidate, who's complaining, or inflating his skills or, ahem, *exaggerating* work experiences. Ultimately, we are compelled to build on each Candidate's individuality because we see each Candidate as a person seeking to better himself or herself. Seeking to make a positive change. It's only seeing them for who they really are that we are able to help a Candidate craft a realistic plan of action, based on unique motivational strategies.

Workforce Development is about understanding a true core of a person and helping them make a career. Workforce Development is personal.

Yes, the concept of humanizing Workforce Development grows in part from my own life, my own history, my own visceral, sometimes painful, experiences, when I actually had to swipe that EBT card. But this also reflects years of study and practical application in the Workforce Development field. I've distilled a dynamic, effective expertise from *all* my experiences! Consequently, I'm starting from an honest place, especially when I find myself sitting across from a Candidate.

I can genuinely, compassionately, counsel a Candidate that it is ok to admit that you've fallen. It's ok to accept and benefit from the guidance and teamwork of ImageWorks' approaches to Workforce Development. I tell our Candidates that success doesn't mean you'll never fail. Success means you've looked failure in the eye and found the teammates, inspiration, and strategies you need to get back in stride again. Success means getting up.

◊ ◊ ◊

At the beginning of my Workforce Development career, I unexpectedly rocketed to success in Miami, Florida, only to plunge into a deep valley, lose money, family, a home. I crashed and burned and wound up back home in D.C., where I had to navigate the difficult season, which led to me needing public assistance and using that EBT card I once circulated to make a major point about resilience.

In Miami, I was really still learning who I am. My rise and fall, when I was a younger woman, brought me to a richer appreciation for the Candidates, and confirmed for me the insight that agencies and legislators can do things better.

ImageWorks started as a part of HeavenSent, an image-consulting firm, then moved into professional development consulting and training at the corporate level.

In 1999, I was attending a networking event. We went around the room introducing ourselves. I said I was an image consultant. The woman who was sitting next to me during introductions later came up to me during the reception.

She was intrigued by what I did. She said image consulting would be 'really good for our welfare-to-work women. What would you do for these women?'

I said I wanted to do a makeover contest. She thought it was a great idea but had to talk to the Executive Director of what was then called the Training and Employment Council. She arranged for me to meet with him. I proposed the makeover contest for women on welfare. My key to the makeover idea? If people didn't *look* the part, they wouldn't get the part! And that remains one of our philosophies today.

Actually, the makeover proposal was rejected by the Council's board of directors. But the executive director came back to me and said, 'There's an RFP out on the street and you should apply.' I had no clue what an RFP was.

I went home and called my best friend, who was a federal government procurement professional. I asked, 'What's an RFP?' She explained the request for proposal process. So I got an opportunity, but I had never done this before. My friend helped me produce my proposal. I submitted it and we were awarded a $35,000 contract.

At the time, I operated HeavenSent out of my house. It still shocks me after all these years. My office was in my second bedroom. Well, the agency staff had to conduct a site visit, before the contract could be executed. I explained that my office was in my home. I was told that my office had to be in a commercial office setting. By the time they came to my home, I had secured a place on Flagler Street in downtown Miami. The same place where they filmed Bad Boys! I got my first contract. In my mind, God said Workforce Development is the field in which I'm supposed to be working, because I certainly had no original knowledge or desire to join the field. I signed the contract in December 1999. By end of the program year, which ran from January-September 30, 2000, ImageWorks had exceeded the original contract value exponentially.

Our program was called Building a Successful Image. In January of 2000, we started with just me as primary trainer; I had a part-time assistant who would handle all the admin stuff. I did all the teaching. Then I met a woman who'd written a book about self-esteem; she allowed HeavenSent to use it as part of our program. Every program participant would get a book. The book's author began teaching self-esteem and I taught the image-development and career planning sections of the curriculum.

During that first year, the company grew from teaching at a single 'One-Stop Center' located in the Liberty City neighborhood to providing services at 11 centers throughout Miami-Dade County. Classes at the centers took place four days a week, six hours a day. The entire program was 24 hours over four days a week, with an average class cohort of 15-18 people. That's how our contract grew. We taught one week per cohort. We had a successful completion rate of over 85 percent. Lives were being changed.

I had never taught before. Never! I had done some corporate training, and most of those workshops were for two hours, maybe a half-day. At that time, we didn't even have a curriculum workbook! Of course, I felt some trepidation at the beginning, but somehow I always felt comfortable in my skin in the classroom. I felt like I was where I was supposed to be.

Every single Monday we had to break the ice with a group of new people. Some were open and with some you knew you had a mountain to climb. We only had four days to develop a relationship with them. We started with self-esteem. That's a hard topic with a group of women you don't know, and who, for the most part, don't know each other.

In Miami, we were training the women on how to change their own 'soft skills'—there's that term again! We taught them how to effectively interview for work. We taught them resume writing. We even taught a *dining tutorial*. Don't laugh! We drilled down to what sounds mundane because we wanted them all to feel powerful in any social setting. We were, of course, helping them develop their image—which clothing best presents a professional image? Dressing them to help build self-esteem. Teaching them that no matter the environment, they would feel more and more comfortable.

Our logic followed the life of a professional: 1. Self-esteem. 2. Resume and interview skills. 3. Networking. 4. Dining skills. Then into Life Skills: How to choose an apartment? Read a lease? How to interview a day care person? How to create and manage a budget. Open a checking account, balance a checkbook.

Our assumption: if you feel better about yourself, you can learn to live a life in which you take care of your kids, get a place to live, go to work. This elemental format is another way that ImageWorks innovatively approaches Workforce Development.

Here's one story that will always remind me that all people deserve an opportunity.

There was an elderly woman in Carol City. She was the oldest person ever in my class. She would come to class every day on time, wearing a housedress. She didn't have a lot of teeth in her mouth. She was receiving welfare because she was taking care of her grandchildren. Both of her daughters were strung out on drugs. She would talk. She would participate in the activities. Flip the pages in the workbook. She took the assessment pre-test, which we put aside till the end of the week.

On the last day, students took the post-test. She came up to me at my desk and asked to see me after class; she said she wanted some help. After class, she said she loved being there, but she did not know how to read. We sat down together. I asked her the questions and she answered them. I don't know if she ever got a job because we weren't required to track those outcomes. But her dedication will inspire me forever.

◊ ◊ ◊

Looking back with hard-earned wisdom, I define myself as someone who became a businessperson, but who had no idea how to run a business!

I spent way too much money—period! Business money. Personal money. We were billing monthly invoices between $30-$50,000! We were making lots of money, but I didn't know how to manage it. I didn't listen to my banker, who said put into your account enough funds to cover 6 months of expenses; an accountant who said you've got to pay yourself a salary. I paid my staff pretty well for a small business; hired Candidates from our classes.

From the outside, everything looked great. I sat on the board of an organization called South Florida Workforce (SFW), and was Chair of its youth council. I also was Chair of the Women's Chamber of Commerce of Miami-Dade County. I was in positions of leadership in organizations around the city. People knew who I was and it felt good.

But in my personal life, and in my mind, I was feeling insecure, based on doubts connected to how I grew up in a working-class household in Washington, D.C.

Even though I was making lot of money—our highest gross was $1.5 million—and was able to buy a house, all of those kinds of things, I wasn't learning those *business* fundamentals. I had only earned an Associates Degree in fashion merchandising; I had no 'business' idea what I was doing.

All I knew was that the program was 'successful' and we were making a difference in people's lives. I had almost totally gotten away from 'true' image consulting. I had a few hardcore clients, but I wasn't able to serve others. I could not manage to solicit other image consulting business, because the Workforce Development work helped the company grow so quickly from that first contract. From 2000 to 2004, the company went from a two-person shop to 15 employees!

It was too much. If I'd been a smarter leader, I would have insisted that we keep seeking corporate training and image-consulting business. That way, I'd have diversified the company's income, instead of relying exclusively on publicly funded Workforce Development contracts, which was a very common mistake for small companies that receive local funds.

I lacked a foundation in business. I hadn't cultivated my ability to view money through a prism, so to speak. My perspective? Money coming in! As in, is there money coming? There is? Then great! I had very little clue about the importance of varied sources of income. I had almost no clue about building contingency into my budgeting. I had a weak savings muscle! My banker would say, 'Carla, you've got to put more money aside.'

I should not have had any issues with payroll. We had a quarter of a million dollar payroll, but we became a cash-poor company—primarily because of my decision-making. In part, the decisions stemmed, and this was positive but shortsighted, from wanting to treat my staff well. For example, our receptionist, who was a former student in my classes (I hired about 3 or 4 students from my classes), was making $25-26,000 a year. It was much more than minimum wage, much more than she had ever made in her life. Our office manager was earning about $40,000 a year; my primary instructor was making about $65,000 a year, after coming on full time. Instructors were paid $15-$18 an hour. I paid myself about $57,000 a year from June/July of 2001 up to 2004.

◊ ◊ ◊

Meanwhile, I also wasn't thoughtfully managing my personal life. I didn't put as much value on the management part as I did in the living part. In 2000, I was just turning 34, when I got that first contract. For the first time in my life, I was able to do what I wanted to do. I didn't have to think about whether or not I could afford it.

I once went to San Francisco for a conference, and I'm walking around Union Square. And I bought a pair of diamond stud earrings for $2,500. Now, I would say no to myself. That's a level of maturity that has come with age, of course, but it also reflects an understanding that you don't have to have everything, even if you can afford it.

◊ ◊ ◊

Looking back, it was like I stood in a glittering valley. I began believing that everything was in place because of what I was doing. I began believing my success was all about what I was doing. I was written up in the paper. Even at the very beginning, I was sending out press releases—I hired a publicist—and news outlets would call for stories about our work. We were all over the paper, including the *Miami Herald*. I really wanted to move back into being an image consultant. And let the Workforce Development be managed by someone else. But I got a taste of the limelight. I started believing, 'Oh my goodness this is me!? The little girl from Southeast D.C.?'

Ultimately, the business began to slide into insolvency. Laws changed. Contracts weren't renewed. A new executive director was taking South Florida Workforce into a new direction. Nonprofits were beginning to get more contracts.

I didn't know how to keep up. And I didn't know how to run a business. All in all, I began making emotional decisions instead of rational ones. When the rubber met the road I did not really know how to sustain myself in a down economy. The tide started turning from mid-2004.

At the same time, my personal life was ruining my concentration, distracting me from problem solving. I ended up divorcing my husband. My life kept getting more and more and more complex. And deep within me, I was feeling toxic self-doubt. I began to realize I needed spiritual help. I had reached the limits of my wisdom.

When I moved to Miami, I gave more focus to my spiritual life. But as the company grew—a company I believe God gave to me—I began focusing more on my efforts and less on the gifts from above. I stopped tithing, and even though I attended church regularly—even the Pastor's wife was a client—I was caught up in my own hype. God has a way of breaking it all down.

During this downward spiral, I returned to my Spirit base. I'd found inner comfort, but I had challenges yet to face. As we continued earning substantial income, I became more visible within Workforce Development circles, and improved my ability to think like a businesswoman. For example, I would put money away on the business side; there was a point that I was taking salary every two weeks. Payroll and bills were being paid on time, enough for me to be approved for the house, car. I had a line of credit for the business.

Today, I am much more humble. I'm smarter knowing that at any moment it can be wiped away. My financial decisions are more calculated. When I look back, I prayed less, tithed less, I made choices that were not based on my prayer life, and I believe that lack of humility is what got in the way of listening. I began believing that everything was in place because of what I was doing, and, as a Believer, I know that ALL good things come from the Lord.

I still don't have all the answers, despite all my experience. Also, I've learned to listen to human colleagues and to messages from the Holy Spirit, a strategic blend that enriches my business tool kit and personal capacities.

I accepted the Lord after I moved to Miami in 1994. I read the Bible. Attended Bible study. When I was studying the Book of Ruth, and her grieving decision to change her name, I was praying, and I heard very clearly the Holy Spirit telling me to change the name of the new company I was starting from StyleLiners to HeavenSent.

Being who I am, I first said, 'You got to be kidding me!' I continued with my plans to stick with StyleLiners, as an homage to my mother. But it kept coming that I needed to call the name of the company HeavenSent. I heeded, finally. After going with the change, I went to a lunch at Miami City Club. It was a networking event for business and professional women. And we're going around the room introducing ourselves. This woman I'm sitting next to, she says she's a partner at Holland and Knight, a law firm. She needed to dress for an upcoming event. I dressed her from head to toe. She looked fabulous. I began dressing other lawyers. The firm became a corporate client—in Miami and D.C.!

For me, it was about obedience. Hear God's voice and heed the direction that I was given. So that I knew obedience is better than sacrifice. Once I was driving, coming down the ramp in Miami, making a left turn. I was at the stoplight, in the middle turn lane. As the light changed, I heard a voice say STOP. I stopped and 30 seconds later a driver going 60 miles an hour raced down the left-turn-only lane. If I had turned left I'd be dead. For me, when you listen you're protected.

Years after rising into my faith, I can now put into words the rite of passage I had to endure during my years in Miami. I was feeling myself. I stopped listening to God. Also, I wasn't tithing as much. My decisions were decisions that were not 'prayed-on decisions,' not spiritually grounded decisions. They were emotional decisions versus spiritually focused decisions.

Although I'm guided and governed by my faith, I, of course, *never* insist that our Candidates follow my faith walk. If a conversation comes up about faith, I will share my belief. I don't shy away from it, but I don't always volunteer it. I tell people that ImageWorks is not a faith-based company but a company based on faith. We're a company whose leadership runs the company based on those principles—I go to church, I read the Bible, I believe in tithing—and that guides the rationales supporting my service to our Candidates. But we're a business dedicated to helping Candidates reach their goals using their *own* principles.

Finally, let me tell you a story about my own mother.

When I was young, and I was going to modeling school—Barbizon, of course. We could only afford to pay the tuition on the 35-dollar-a-week plan. She paid. She and my father paid. My sister-in-law paid. I remember asking my mother:

'If I were a twin and we both wanted to go, how would we do it?'

That's something a 13-year-old would say.

She said, 'I don't know, but we would figure it out! Whatever it takes!'

I think everybody should have a mother (*or even a Workforce Development mother!*) who co-signs what they really, really want to do. Chasing your goals, achieving your goals, generates powerful personal illuminations and breakthroughs and can cause ripple effects.

On the positive side: more children would grow up believing that they could do whatever they want. That it's ok to dream. Ok to find what you want to do and find someone to support you. For me, with few exceptions, I have never done any other kind of work ever. I've worked retail. Sold high-end clothes. I became an expert at all these things, because I had interest in it as a kid. ImageWorks today is the grown-up version of that interest and support.

Conversely, if loved ones don't support children, don't encourage them, that, too, has a ripple effect. They don't believe in themselves. They don't feel that their desire has any merit. They can end up living a life that's ebbing and flowing and moving moment-to-moment.

Let me put it another way. Let's look at what I'm saying through the lens of Workforce Development. And I view this as one of ImageWorks' innovations. Besides supporting a Candidate's dreams, we also get down to the nuts and bolts of reaching those dreams.

We teach Candidates to be methodical, to be intentional. We teach Candidates to stay conscious of what it is they really want to do at all times throughout the Workforce Development process. We help them learn to work backwards. Whatever their end-goal is, work backwards and itemize the steps needed to take the journey towards the end-goal.

Remember the Candidate who wanted to be a Nurse?

To be nurse, you have to go to school. You may have to go all the way back to school. Maybe you only have a year-and-a-half of college. First, you have to go back to get that first degree; then you have to go to nursing school. Now, let's say that as an employee, all you have today are administrative skills. So now, you come to ImageWorks. I say, 'OK, your end-goal is be a nurse. Tell me what kind of work you have done. Ahh, you've worked as an admin for demanding lawyers.' I say to my Candidate: 'if you were successful in that work, it means you work very well under pressure. How much pressure will it take to go back to school? To continue to provide for your family?' That's the mental part of it.

Then there's the logistical part. Where do you have to go to school? How much does it cost? When do you have to register for classes? Are you able to get money to go? You have to have internal skills to manage the logistics, but I'll remind her that she's used all of the necessary skills, except in a different role with the lawyers. And I'll teach her to transfer her law-office skills over to managing the steps she must take to reach her dream of becoming a nurse.

But if the Candidate's mind is closed, she can only see herself in the place she's in when she walks through the doors at ImageWorks!

We help Candidates remove barriers and start thinking bigger. We help them see themselves taking methodical steps to get where they want to go. Being methodical means writing it down, affirming those steps. Yes, make an actual list. Create actual timelines. Putting the pieces in place through research, through constantly affirming—because there are going to be some haters. Then once the Candidate gets into school there's a whole new set of steps. You have to do it in bite-size chunks.

This contrasts, unfortunately, with how too many Workforce Development agencies operate.

For the most part, agency funding is based on performance. Performance is defined as who gets a job and getting that job at what wage is determined by where you live. The ultimate IS THE JOB for Workforce Development agencies! The ultimate is to get a job. ANY JOB.

I want them to move into a career. You might have to get some jobs to get the career, but the end-goal is to have a career.

The BASICS of Divine Wisdom

Excerpts from Carla's Journal Entries

INTERLUDE

Dear Heavenly Father: I owe You an apology. I am sorry for all the times I wanted to do things my way and not follow Your guidance. You would think that every time I get in the way, things really mess up. You may be wondering when things are back on track will I move back to doing it my way. Actually, You don't wonder. You already know. I hope I know even in the smallest crevice of my mind that I am truly nothing without You. No matter what I try, if I do it without You, I will fail. As I sit here this evening, I still do not see, but I am trusting You. You have arranged it so that I have no device but to trust You. All my wells have dried up and I don't mean to be nonchalant, I just see You in this and I know You will provide. I lost my faith Lord. I began driving more for me than for You; sometimes, I feel like You hid Your face from me, so I would seek You earnestly. I am not certain what You have for my life; I just know I am willing to find out. I have come very close to allowing You to have complete control and then I take over. But not this time. This time I want to go all the way. I ask myself why I stop and my only conclusion is fear. Trepidation. Apprehension. Whatever it's called, it all equals fear. I am turning my fear over to You. I am falling back with the full knowledge that You will catch me.

EMOTIONAL INTELLIGENCE & IMAGEWORKS' BASIC PROGRAM

We use a Candidate's innate desires, abilities and interests to guide the career pathway planning process. Workforce preparation activities are keenly focused on a guided combination of passion, self-awareness, critical thinking, emotional intelligence, and problem solving skills. These skills are sorely missing in many Candidates.

The Building a Successful Image for Change (BASIC) program is used for career awareness, readiness and exploration for all Candidates. The BASIC program is an 8-week program that addresses the professional development skills needed for success in any workplace. Work preparation activities include developing 'emotional intelligence,' improving the ability to communicate effectively, understanding cultural diversity and the need to be sensitive to others, critical thinking and problem solving.

According to employers, these skills are glaringly missing from Workforce Development Candidates, yet are critical to their success in the workplace. The skills, abilities and traits that pertain to personality, attitude and behavior, rather than to formal or technical knowledge, are critical to address in a program that serves people with limited work experience. These skills are among employers' most important hiring criteria and account for many of the reasons that new workers lose their jobs. Most damaging for Candidates? Lack of emotional intelligence, or the ability to stay aware of emotions, manage their behavior and tendencies, and understand other people's moods, behavior, and motives. We have found that Candidates must learn to not take things personally and to maintain self-control.

We help Candidates develop and strengthen their 'emotional intelligence' through exercises that hone self-management skills that teach them to govern emotions in the workplace; separate personal and home life from the workplace and vice/versa; 'unhook' from toxic relationships; and maintain a better grasp that self-awareness and self-knowledge equals a better understanding of workplace expectations.

Humanizing Policy

Humanizing Policy

"You can't humanize policy," he shouted out during a brainstorming session in a workshop at ImageWorks' Hiring from the Sidelines conference for Workforce Development and Social Services Professionals in Washington, D.C. in October of 2017.

His comment struck a chord for the workshop facilitator, who wrote it on the big sheet of paper he'd stuck to the wall to track comments from participants. The comment led to workshop participants collectively grappling with the implications of their colleague's assertion. Ironically, the comment surfaced during day two of three days of rich, thoughtful discussion about how to 'humanize' Workforce Development work on behalf of Candidates and their families.

Besides contributing to conference discussions, the comment offered a challenge to examine even more closely the Workforce Innovation and Opportunity Act (WIOA), the federal law governing the country's Workforce Development framework.

After a refresher review of WIOA, I came away reinvigorated! The dry, legalese of the Act actually strengthens my rationale for humanizing human services.

How?

We must approach Workforce *services* with the same systematic rigor that states and municipalities, nonprofits and vendors must employ for meeting what the Act calls "fiscal control and fund accounting procedures."

How could we establish a 'service' version of "fiscal control and fund accounting procedures that may be necessary to ensure the proper disbursement of, and accounting for, funds paid to the State through allotments made for adult, dislocated worker[s], and youth programs to carry out workforce investment activities. [SEC. 102.,]"

In other words, from policy makers to professional staff, from accounting departments to boards of directors, nobody doubts that *effective* organizations must carefully follow the legal requirements for accounting how public funds are managed and spent.

My question is how can those same Workforce professionals doubt that an effective organization should know how to treat the folks who require our assistance? The folks we're paid (via public funds) to assist?

Think creatively with me. Track public money? Of course. Ensure fiscal compliance? You better believe it. Use familiar, agreed-upon tools? Indeed. Realistic, well-managed budgets. Balance Sheets. Notes that explain changing fiscal rationales or anomalies.

Bear with me, now. Let's think about *how* we provide services for which we're paid by public funds.

What tools track the character and quality of our service to Candidates? Could they be made uniform? Could they be incorporated into intake assessments of Candidates? Could they help deepen our relationships with Candidates?

What if our funding levels were tied to the quality of our relationships with our Candidates, in addition to finding them work?

Oh, we would then surely 'humanize policy!' And our services!

Think I'm crazy?! Think this has nothing to do with getting a 'client' a job?

Well, WIOA targets 'adult, dislocated worker[s], and youth' and seeks "to increase, for individuals in the United States, particularly those individuals with barriers to employment, access to and opportunities for the employment, education, training, and support services they need to succeed in the labor market."

Translation: WIOA governs services to citizens who are, by definition, in crisis, in transition, wracked with doubts, under court supervision, returning from incarceration.

Which Candidates need the 'human touch' more?

How can organizations help such Candidates succeed without first 'embracing' their humanity?

What services could possibly 'stick' without viewing such Candidates as partners?

We must absolutely get more rigorously humane in our systems, our policies. Not by *distancing* ourselves and saying that policy is policy and service is service. Not by distancing ourselves from the very real challenges we all face—Candidates and service providers alike. But by infusing our work with more common sense and inspiration.

I concede that we must often demand change from our Candidates. But also, we must demand change from ourselves.

Let me itemize what I consider the basics of how ImageWorks works with our Candidates. Even beyond "Best Practices," let me suggest these as bedrock fundamentals to humanizing Workforce Development policies.

Workforce Professionals must become active listeners, in addition to being experts dispensing counsel and directives.

Workforce Professionals must view their time and interactions as respectful investments combined with clearly stated objectives in language completely understood by Candidates.

Workforce Professionals must define services as constructive tools that build the capacity of Candidates—not as charity, nor handouts.

Workforce Professionals must craft dynamic partnerships with Candidates and assist them in articulating attainable goals.

Workforce Professionals must, finally, provide a context specific to each Candidate that answers elemental questions, such as: How can I transmit to my children and other family members new standards, patterns, goals, and practical strategies?

Ultimately, it's not either policy or humanizing. WIOA uses terms such as "System Alignment," "Self Sufficiency," "One-stop Delivery System,"—our job is to define what those terms mean in the dynamic, difficult, deeply human interactions with living Candidates.

We must understand that without humane interaction with Candidates policy is empty. Empty policy leads to lack of effectiveness. Ineffectiveness leads to legislators reducing or eliminating funding. And that leaves us *ALL* as failures.

Let me put this to a test by using the WIOA language governing State Workforce Development Boards. According to the Act, the boards must ensure the "development and continuous improvement of the one-stop delivery system; the development of strategies to support staff training and awareness across programs supported under the Workforce Development system; the development and updating of comprehensive State performance accountability measures, including State adjusted levels of performance, to assess the effectiveness of the core programs in the State ...; the identification and dissemination of information on best practices, including best practices [for] effective operation ... development of effective local boards ... effective training programs ... [and to] strengthen the professional development of providers and workforce professionals...."

That's not literature. I think we can agree on that. Of course, I don't expect a federal law to read like a novel, or a poem, or a Hallmark card about the quality of human communications.

But WIOA's language still offers me opportunities to 'humanize policy,' if I'm guided by my experience in the trenches.

And I argue that if other social service professionals, who *have* been educated and trained to be close observers of human behavior, shift their perspectives, they, too, can also place at the center of providing services the very humanity of Candidates, and their very human circumstances.

If I draw out terms from the Act, while imagining a Candidate sitting right in front of me, then I can write a mission statement that goes something like this:

ImageWorks prioritizes the unique needs of Workforce Candidates and serves their 'continuous improvement' by helping them create 'development of strategies' leading to secure employment as part of their journey to a self-sufficient lifestyle. Also, ImageWorks provides 'staff training,' which increases 'awareness' that Candidates are the central focus of Workforce services; ensures mutual 'development' and 'effectiveness'; and empowers mutual 'identification and dissemination of information on best practices;' that 'strengthen the professional development of providers and workforce professionals' and Candidates.

Put in the succinct language of a mission statement, 'humanizing policy' doesn't seem so counter-intuitive. Nor does it seem like an impossibility. Such a mission provides guidance for serving Candidates in the emergency-fueled, stressful ecology of Workforce Development. It values and *prioritizes* taking time to fully *engage* with a Candidate's humanity in a deliberate, yet rigorously systematic set of sequential processes that build on the initial intake application and assessment.

Absent a revised mission statement, too often Workforce Development leaders push professional staff to speed up. And what happens? Often we prioritize a particularly angry or disruptive Candidate, and push him or her to the 'front of the line.' There goes the deliberate, yet rigorously systematic set of sequential processes!

At its best, that tendency to jump-start the process for a Candidate could mean staff is simply trying to help someone faster. At its worst, given the stresses of Workforce Development, sped-up staff are cruising for burnout by scrambling to oil the squeaky wheels of each person's currently dysfunctional situation.

An alternative?

Cultivate the biggest picture. Build into our work the biggest picture. Let's stop matching dysfunction for dysfunction, which raises the stress for all parties involved. Nobody benefits when staff feels as overwhelmed as the Candidates.

Furthermore, this new mission statement would liberate experienced Workforce Development staff to lead with their expertise. After years of working with Candidates, they possess the well-honed ability to discern the 'fingerprints' of each Candidate's circumstances. Under the right mission statement, and supported by policy makers and organizational leadership, they have the ability to carve out the amount of time with Candidates that appropriately creates a more effective ecology of service and success.

The new mission frees us to establish procedures that *build into each interaction* the particular amount of time required to serve a given Candidate, in order to break the circuit of their emergency.

And turn the discussion and planning and actions toward each Candidate reaching WIOA's "eligible outcomes—employment, retention, independence and earnings."

Not to mention WIOA's vaunted goal of 'Self Sufficiency.'

WIOA mentions the words 'self-sufficiency' 23 times. However, nowhere is the term defined. State and local agencies must determine their own definition based on its own terms. Often none take into account the psychological impact that poverty has on our Candidates. Humanizing a policy goal of self-sufficiency takes more than a Candidate gaining employment.

It goes without saying that we need *one* cohesive, national definition of self-sufficiency. Social workers, case managers and job coaches are keenly aware of the program requirements for gaining and retaining employment.

Without rigorously humanized procedures, however, much of that retention is lost due to a Candidate's lack of ability to handle what can be an overwhelming life filled with demanding children, choosing between food and clothing, and failing to discern the intangible strengths they need to move themselves forward.

The new mission statement above would empower us to take the time to help Candidates *change their perspective about their situations.*

For example:

They are facing temporary challenges, which can be solved, and are not permanent barriers for the rest of their lives.

Challenges can be looked at as puzzles, or as beginnings, or as tests. They don't have to be problems, traps or dead-ends.

Workforce Candidates are not weak, lazy victims. They are human beings in a temporary crisis, who have the intelligence, imagination and potential to be partners with Workforce Professionals in the resolution of their challenges.

Candidates are citizens who have the *right* to benefit from training, coaching, and opportunities.

By coming to us for help, they have taken the first powerful step to weather their crises, then learn how to empower themselves to create and execute a plan, while joining forces with others to contribute to all areas of life—work, family and community.

That's self-sufficiency. That's 'humanizing policy.'

Workforce Development helps Candidates realize that they are *deserving* and *worthy* of moving themselves and their families forward and helps to make the transition from government assistance to self-sufficiency.

It's not magic. It's human beings serving human beings.

The Power to be The Best: The Courage to be You

Excerpt of a speech by Carla Harris to Baltimore County Department of Human Resources staff graduation, 2017.

For the past 20 years I've been in business, the peaks have been very high and the valleys have been very low…and such is life. So today, as you move into another milestone, I want to congratulate you. Each step you take to better your future can be easy or hard, but sometimes they are steps you must take. Taking classes is not required to keep your job, but the desire to improve yourself is required if you want to move to the next level.

Just like you, I knew I wanted to be the best. Be the best in business. Be the best in the community I served. And be the best personally…for me. I've discovered that being the best sometimes takes courage. It's easy to give our all, but as we move up the ladder of success, we have to remember the courage it takes to remain true to ourselves. To not bend to the whims of others. It takes courage to fail. Courage to maintain integrity. It takes courage to succeed without selling your soul to the devil.

As you continue to grow in your career, I want to share with you six lessons I've learned over the years.

1. You are not your best motivator. We all have 2 voices in our heads—the good and the bad …sort of the angel and the devil sitting on your shoulder. Depending on many factors, the bad voice can shout a little louder than the good one. Surround yourself with others who have your best interest at heart and who can see in you what you cannot see in yourself.

   Strong, successful businesses have a board of directors, a group of people who remain objective about where the company is going. You need that. **Create a board of directors for yourself**. It doesn't have to be a large board, but it does have to be a strong board. A group of people you trust and whose opinion is grounded in what's best for you. These are the people who will mentor you, cheer you on, and call you on the carpet when needed. Choose people who are honest, kind and inspired to see you be the best you can be.

2. **Don't view yourself through the lens of others.** Rest assured, there will be others who want to bring you down...slow your progress... distract you. Don't let them. See yourself through the lens of faith and your ability to conquer the world. See yourself through the lens of your strength and desire to be the best you can be.

Letting others define who you are robs you of the power you have within.

Letting others define who you are robs you of the power you have within. During my divorce, my ex-husband said to the judge... "it's just a little company I helped my wife start..." I thought about those words on the day I read an article about my company in the *Miami Herald* newspaper...

Times will get tough.

Decisions need to be made.

And, sometimes, you may have to fire some folks in your life.

3. **How you do anything is how you do everything.** I coach long term unemployed job seekers as part of our Workforce Development program and many of them say they "won't act this way when they get on the job..." And my response is always, "yes, you will!" **Who you are is who you are**. No matter where you are. Think about that. Whether at work, home or with friends, who you are is who you are. So, if you give it your best at home, you will give it your best at work. And contrary, if mediocrity is acceptable in one area of your life, it will be acceptable in all areas of your life.

4. **It takes courage to be you.** As teenagers, it's very hard not to buckle to peer pressure. As we grow into mature, emotionally

intelligent adults, we learn to stand our ground, be true to our convictions and to maintain integrity in all we do. As you climb the ladder of success, be courageous in your opinion. Have the gumption to speak out against what's wrong. Live by the standards you have set for yourself.

5. **Relationships begin with giving**. Networking is key to any successful career. Many people attend networking events and want to develop working relationships—all for the wrong reasons.

　　To get something.

　　Relationships begin with providing a genuine interest in others. One of my mentors once told me that you must first give to get. Share an article that's of interest. Ask about their career...their family...their likes. Begin developing a professional friendship and the business will come. People do business with people they like.

6. **Falling doesn't mean failing**. First, we crawl, then we walk, then we run. Falling is a part of life. Get up! And get up again! There are many who have fallen...

　　Bill Gates—Dropped out of college.

　　Michael Jordan was cut from his high school basketball team.

　　Oprah Winfrey was fired from her first news anchor job at age 22.

　　Beyonce, in her first girl group, lost on national TV.

The list goes on...The failure is not in falling but is in *not getting up*.

Be a LION...even on those days when you really want to be a kitty.

Be a soldier...even if you are the only one on the front line.

And finally, be KIND. Because kindness is the oil that will take the friction out of life.

Congratulations on your endeavors, I know you have many more to come. Thank you for allowing me to be a part of your celebration. God bless each of you.

A GLOSSARY NOTE

WIOA provides legal definitions of terms used by Workforce Development policy makers and industry professionals. These definitions delineate what needs to be done and who needs to be served. As part of its 'Humanizing Human Services Project,' ImageWorks has begun changing the definitions of key terms. See the chart below. It focuses on two key areas. How could other terms be changed?

From	To
Participant, client or customer	**CANDIDATE** Employers hire Candidates; they don't hire participants or clients. Using the term Candidate not only increases the level of respect from provider to recipient, but also increases the value with which the Candidate see themselves. Additionally, it increases the value of the relationship between the employer and the Workforce Professional referring the Candidate for the job.
Workforce Development	**PROFESSIONAL DEVELOPMENT** Professionals get coaching; we have mentors; we continue our professional growth. In the corporate world when employees or job seekers need to brush up on their skills, it's called *professional development training*. It's the same for our Candidates.

CHAPTER FIVE

Courage to Change

Courage to Change

Innovation puts you ahead of the curve. Ideas such as Humanizing Social Services or Humanizing Workforce Policy are difficult to explain, and difficult to execute in the heat of RFPs, resolving the emergencies of Candidates, and analyzing how to apply and synchronize best practices in publicly funded agencies.

Frankly, seeking to innovate can lead to difficult conversations, lost colleagues, reduced contracts or loss of contracts. Innovation is no joke. It shakes us up. It forces all involved to confront change. To find the courage to change.

Boy do I get it! Translating my vision for myself, for policy leaders, agency staff—well, that's part of the reason for writing *FaithWorks*.

Since I began my Workforce Development career, I've had to adapt and change. I've had to adapt to my mistakes. I've had to change in order to better serve Candidates.

As I seek to grow ImageWorks, to remain strategic, I am now blending priorities. I envision the best way to serve Candidates is to influence the structures governing how Candidates are served. Train the trainers.

My focus is taking me toward figuring out how to educate the providers on how to treat people. Educate and consult with companies on how to hire from this group of Candidates.

In previous chapters, I've outlined how strongly I believe in the people we serve at ImageWorks. How critical it is to 'humanize' Workforce Development by *truly* placing the men, women and children we serve at the very center of our work. Even beyond common sense, I've argued that this approach actually *activates* WOIA.

I've plunged myself into new ways of thinking. I'm taking new angles in order to provide effective services. I've very strategically begun changing ImageWorks.

In short, this evolution has led to creation of ImageWorks' new training academy—The People Institute, through which we will provide professional development to all current and future employees, Candidates, and clients.

The term 'Workforce Development' serves to further the separation between mainstream and marginalized Candidates. Guess what? There is no difference.

Each is seeking to be employed. Words are powerful. When you're out of work, you're marginalized by definition—until you get back up on your feet!

◊ ◊ ◊

As we gear up The People Institute, let me close by meditating briefly on change.

In the best of times, leadership demands sacrifice. But making sacrifices in challenging times reveals that you've learned to make mature changes.

Unlike in the past, I can more quickly discern and recognize important signs. I make conscious decisions that don't rest on emotions.

ImageWorks will continue to provide our umbrella, but The People Institute puts our philosophy in the title! I'm making real changes based on what's right for the company, what's right for me. I'm excited to execute what I counsel my Candidates to do. Be very clear in your thinking. Feel very clear in your decisions.

Make changes that reflect your clarity and stand on your faith.

Every time I make a professional change, a life change, I think about the Candidates I serve and have served over the years.

How many changes do they have to make?

How much does their decision impact their children?

Their household?

Change is hard. In business. In life.

Change shows me that I've learned something. I've learned from my mistakes. You don't wait until the well is completely dry to make a decision. I don't have to repeat. It's an inspiring revelation for me. Remembering that change is constant.

◊ ◊ ◊

I'm taking ImageWorks from the trenches into a mid-level tower. Just like our Candidates, I am pivoting.

When I was taught to model, and had to make a turn, we were taught to pivot. Very intentional. Now it's nothing for me to turn on a dime even, if I'm walking down the street. It becomes a part of who you are. A pivot is more intentional than transition.

Teaching our Candidates to pivot is teaching them to be more intentional with their actions, their thoughts, and their goals. Making intentional living a part of who they are.

I'm also asking the field of Workforce Development to pivot.

We must become more intentional with our actions, thoughts and goals. We must have faith in the men, women and children we serve. And we must work.

I call it FaithWorks. I know our society will be better for it.

Jumpstarting Organizational Change

Especially Our Goal to 'Train the Trainers'

INTERLUDE

From our Fall 2017 conference, Hiring from the Sidelines, to staff development workshops with Baltimore County Department of Human Resources, to strategic collaborations with nonprofits such as the Salvation Army, I'm leveraging ImageWorks' experience and innovative approaches to Workforce Development, especially our goal to 'train the trainers.' Also, we're better using on-line platforms to succinctly promote our programs and initiatives. We've distilled our thinking, and so crystallized our strengths, that I can confidently promise that if an organization gives us *one hour* we can jumpstart organizational change. One example that illustrates our powerful pivot is this link to ImageWorks' Lunch & Learn Video: https://www.youtube.com/watch?v=x_FdrFVhXzc

THE GRITT APPROACH: AN IMAGEWORKS & INSPIRATION HOUSE COLLABORATION

Guide (w/) **R**igor an **I**ndividual('s) **T**alent **T**ransformation

... is a tool for 'Strategic Circuit Breaking' that Workforce Development professionals, Arts Education staff and students, and Community Stakeholders can use to illuminate and examine intersections where personal and social change occurs, then craft plans to negotiate with, and influence, governmental decision-making, high-stakes economics, and important public policies.

... demystifies change through rigorous examination of the powerful interpersonal and social forces such as gentrification, demographic shifts, and economic inequality, while simultaneously showing that inspirational storytelling can be combined with Individual fortitude and determination to forge the foundation for renewal and confidence that creativity and imagination are indispensable tools for constructive personal and social change.

... allows for a dynamic, 3-dimensional review of change through such critical, incisive questions as: *What interpersonal and social forces govern major, on-going social transformations? What could I learn from the leaders of transformative changes? What role do I want to play in future changes? How can I learn from leaders of billion dollar projects? What changes must I make to get where I want to go? What can I learn from my past decisions? How will my past actions hurt or help in the making of my most positive tomorrow? What jobs do I see? What jobs do I not see?*

... lifts human and social development 'off the page' by reminding us that ALL humans can influence major change, even those who've been marginalized and made to feel they can only be spectators as the gears of the future grind right before their eyes.

... targets the epicenters of dynamic change to expand borders and visions, enrich analyses with strategic creativity, and positions ALL humans to both personally improve their lives and align their tomorrows with the brightest futures they can imagine.

... is inspired by—and incorporates—the book *GRITT TUFF Play Book, written* by humanitarian Glenn Harris, Emmy-winning member of the DC Sports Hall of Fame; and American Book Award-winning writer Peter J. Harris, Founding Director of Inspiration House and the Black Man of Happiness Project.

The ImageWorks' Vision

CONCLUSION

The ImageWorks' Vision

Workforce Development demands that we walk several tightropes all at the same time.

Humanizing Human Services—the core of ImageWorks' Workforce Development vision—demands we *dance ballet* on those tightropes!

I use the tightrope image to help you imagine and feel the vertigo that comes with seeking to serve men and women—and our society—by helping them to find sustainable employment and/or a satisfying career.

Let me first capture what it's like to walk the 'big picture' tightrope:

As we work in the field, we must walk the tightrope of federal, state and local laws, rules and regulations. We can easily lose our balance in the crosswinds of the expectations, customs and attitudes of lawmakers, policy analysts, rule-makers, organizational leadership, and staff.

We can lose our balance with the change of a political administration, with the firing of a general manager, after a new staff person's interpretation of a policy or a rule.

Then we have to walk the tightrope between us and the 'Candidates' we serve.

When working with Candidates, we must walk the tightrope of their experiences, attitudes, and personal capacities. We can easily lose our balance in the crosswinds of their unique (but often predictable) responses to social circumstances, the 9-5-needs of an entry-level job, their big, but currently unattainable, dreams, and the demands we place upon them.

And then for some Candidates, whose potential shines, whose dedication promises solid outcomes, we must help them maintain balance against the powerful undertow of dysfunctional family and community histories—indeed even the histories of our country itself.

For us at ImageWorks, we're walking an even more intimate tightrope.

In our work, we're feeling the crosswinds—if not blowback—between the very conceptions at the root of our work and the work of the field itself. Maintaining balance on this tightrope, in my opinion, provides us with the most robust opportunities for the transformative work that will benefit society in far-reaching ways and that will enrich opportunities for us all.

What do I mean by the conceptions at the root of our work?

First, let's start with the folks we serve.

They are not 'clients' but human beings, neighbors, deserving the support of Workforce Development funds and services. Of course, we can see that they are human beings! But do we see them as *deserving* human beings? *Valuable* human beings? Human beings worthy of renewed opportunities after the mistakes or challenges in their lives?

Too often, when we say 'clients' we reduce our neighbors to bloodless statistics. I understand the need for administrative systems that accurately track 'clients.' I understand that when working with 'populations' in transition—from prison, from poverty, from downsizing—public agencies must accurately manage data associated with those 'populations.'

But after we track folks on our servers, we must get beyond data to humanized human services!

We must create an atmosphere in which 'clients' and 'populations' become fellow citizens for whom it's our pleasure to offer effective service.

They cannot in any way shape or form sense that our systems, our personalities, our temperaments, view them as lazy failures or criminals with no hope of redemption, or stubborn workers who don't have the abilities or attitudes necessary to manage our changing economy—from manufacturing to services, from analog to digital, for example.

We have to imagine walking in their shoes. Indeed, haven't we at some point in our lives needed services from our church? Our neighbors? Our government?

And frankly, no matter the economic or political climate, we can treat Candidates with respect. We can be dynamically courteous and patient with Candidates, no matter who's in the White House, the Governor's Mansion, or City Hall.

We must infuse our work with enthusiasm. With creativity. With imagination. With a willingness to roll with the dynamic difficulties embedded in this work. We may have to follow the laws, but we don't have to follow formulas and scripts when we serve the unique needs of the man or woman with whom we are engaged.

Think about it!

WE *HAVE* A JOB when we're communicating with folks facing their worst-case scenarios.

WE HAVE A WORKFORCE DEVELOPMENT JOB, for goodness sake!

It's our J-O-B to help folks find work that can help them live their lives with dignity.

And we're only ON THE JOB when we are effectively, successfully, *developing* the human being, and helping them to identify, refine, and strengthen their capacities to think, plan, discern, prioritize and otherwise gain mastery of their lives.

What body language are we displaying during our conversations with Candidates? What is our tone of voice? Are we making eye contact? Is our language affirming? Or is it wishing we could complete this exchange as quickly as we can!

Can we honestly say we're embodying *encouragement, possibilities, hopefulness?*

And what about our larger office environments?

Is our office a welcoming space? What subsonic message is our receptionist communicating? In what colors are the walls painted? Are the seats comfortable? Is there enough light in the room? Can a Candidate grab a cup of water, or tea, or coffee? Does the place feel like a prison or some other place of incarceration?

Your answers will let me know if you're *humanizing human services!*

Also, let's not get intimidated by the idea of transformation, which I admit rings in our ears like a HUGE idea. I get it. Transforming Workforce Development sounds even more daunting. I do understand.

But what's HUGE from the outside, is actually the application of a series of simple, strategically mapped, approaches and processes— especially if we ask ourselves: *What's best for the person we're serving?*

As I've revealed in the pages of FaithWorks, I've sat on either side of the Workforce Development equation. As service provider. As Candidate. I've spent hours in prayer. I've observed the full scope of Workforce Development practices.

Building on powerful experiences, I now understand my prime mission to be the change I'm advocating.

Going forward, ImageWorks will synthesize the best practices of our field into summaries and outlines and lesson plans to enrich our principles, processes and service to human services leadership, staff and, of course, to Candidates—our neighbors in transition.

ImageWorks will convene conferences and other public engagement programs to allow for fruitful conversation and professional exchanges. We will live-stream interviews with thought leaders. We will produce on-line workshops and webinars to build our capacities.

With these and other programs and events, we will build a bedrock of fundamentals and principles that anchor the most humane approaches to fulfilling our human service missions.

We can learn from each other to refine all that we do with one goal in mind: effective and efficient engagements that affirm the humanity and value of all Candidates and apply our expertise on behalf of their Workforce Development needs.

I will ensure that ImageWorks walks the talk of humanizing human services. Our reputation will ring clear as a bell. Our Candidates, our fellow Workforce Development professionals, will view us as the standard, as the source for a bracing, creative vision that blends the practical with the inspirational.

And here let me make sure you know how much I respect—and learn from—my many fellow professionals in the field of Workforce Development. I do not want them to think my vision for our field is simply *hateration* or indiscriminate criticism.

In fact, I am absolutely clear, and I know for sure, that many human service professionals are *already* providing humane service to Candidates. And all of them believe they are working according to the demands of the law and policies governing our work.

I am thrilled that for years I have collaborated effectively with more amazing Workforce Development professionals than I can count! In Miami, as I began my career, and in the DMV, I have executed contracts with them, sat on policy boards with many of them, discussed the pros and cons of our field with many of them.

No doubt, in my experience, I have been a witness to the deep sense of service that very much motivates and drives the men and women who have chosen to work in the field of Workforce Development.

Yet, I am equally confident that my colleagues share my belief that our field, like so many closed systems, has come to a crossroads, an era that calls for a jolt of inspiration to keep us from resting on our laurels, or getting stuck in patterns, or other practices that are more rut than groove.

I am sure that my colleagues can feel that the times in which we currently live call for us to focus new creative attention to all levels of our operations. During these times, we must snap to attention, trace and address the powerful impacts of rising income inequality, homelessness, transitions of men and women returning from prison and court supervision, the needs of mature Candidates. We must inject ourselves and our work with new urgency, more dynamic strategies, more supple analyses.

I am driven beyond criticism—of individuals, of a given law or policy, of a given agency—to crafting and executing a vision.

My vision rests on a profound sense of connection to the men and women who need us as savvy collaborators, if not friends; who need us as imaginative professionals, if not missionaries; who need us as persistent advocates, if not mentors.

This is my calling.

I am inspired.

I am changed.